Panzer-Division 1935-1945

(3) War on Two Fronts 1943-1945

Text by Robert Michulec
Edited by Tom Cockle
Color plates by Arkadiusz Wròbel

Losses suffered by the Panzer-Divisions during the very long campaign during the last part of 1943 and the turn of 1944 were very high, higher in fact than during Operation 'Citadel'. Retreating from Russia, the Panzer-Divisions lost not only those vehicles totally written off in combat, but also most of the damaged ones that could not be retrieved and repaired as the battlefield belonged to the enemy. On the Italian Front, the controlled withdrawal situation made recovery easier than on the Eastern Front as massive Soviet attacks often resulted in German positions being overrun.

By June 1944, when D-Day officially opened up the second front in Europe, the Germans had lost almost 7,500 tanks and self-propelled guns since the previous summer. This was enough combat vehicles to fully equip 35 Panzer-Divisions. In 1943, production soared under the guidance of Albert Speer, and almost 25,000 new vehicles were built to replace the losses. Decimated Panzer-Divisions were rebuilt and re-equipped so that none ceased to exist, except for 18.Panzer-Division, which was deactivated and reorganized as 18.Artillerie-Division in late October 1943. The 6., 19., and 25.Panzer-Divisions were severely mauled in the fall of 1943 and in the spring of 1944, they were returned to Germany to rest and refit. Others suffered serious losses, but could be re-equipped without withdrawing them completely from combat. In many cases, the high losses resulted from inadequate supplies and not the skill of the defenders. In truth, the average new Panzer soldier was not as well trained as his predecessors from the 1941-42 period, but he was characterized by high morale and determination and was led by a core of competent and experienced officers.

After the battle at Kursk was finally over in August, Only five Heeres Panzer-Divisions and one SS-Panzer-Division were sent as replacements to the Eastern Front in October and November of 1943. Of these, only 1.SS-Panzer-Division LSSAH and 1.Panzer-Division were full strength divisions with two battalions totaling about 200 tanks. The other three, 14., 24. and 25.Panzer-Divisions, had about 100 tanks and assault guns in one single battalion each. There were some other smaller units of battalion and company size that were sent bringing the total strength up to the level of the summer. Between September 1 and December 31, 1943, all units on the Eastern Front averaged 2,000 tanks, of which only 800 were combat ready at any one time. A small force indeed, for such a large front.

During this time in Italy, there were only two Panzer-Divisions along with a few Panzer-Grenadier-Divisions and independent Tiger battalions. The terrain in Italy was completely different from that in the Soviet Union and the use of large scale tank formations was not practical. After the Italian armistice, five Panzer-Divisions were concentrated there to ensure orderly disarmament of the Italian Army and to guard against any armed insurrection by the population. When the danger passed, these were quickly transferred. At this time, most of the Panzer-Divisions were concentrated on the Eastern Front.

An Allied invasion of France was inevitable, and several Panzer-Divisions were stationed there to meet the threat. Among them were some new Panzer-Divisions established in 1943 and early 1944. It was decided that the men and officers of the reserve and training divisions would be absorbed into these divisions. By sacrificing the Panzerwaffe reserves, the establishment and rebuilding of a few new Panzer-Divisions was made possible. Panzer-Lehr-Division, 116.Panzer-Division and 12.SS-Panzer-Division 'Hitlerjugend' appeared in France and in Italy, Panzer-Regiment Hermann Göring was reorganized from a Panzer-Grenadier-Regiment.

In early June 1944, the Germans had nine Panzer-Divisions in France with 1,673 tanks and assault guns, sixteen Panzer-Divisions in Russia with 1,390 and two Panzer-Divisions in Italy with about 350. The 6. and 19.Panzer-Divisions were in Germany being rested and refitted.

By the end of August 1944, the Allies had virtually destroyed the Panzer-Divisions concentrated in the West while many of the Panzer-Divisions in the East suffered high losses as a result of the Soviet summer offensive. The combined cost of the summer campaigns was enormous to the Germans. A total of 2,283 tanks and 1,684 self-propelled guns and 531 Panzerjäger were lost, 4,489 vehicles altogether. No less than 697 were lost in June alone. How serious these losses were, especially to those Panzer-Divisions on the Western Front, is apparent when we learn from reports after the war that by late August, the combined strength of all these units amounted to just over 70 tanks and assault guns which would indicate that over 1,600 of these vehicles had been lost. But much more than just the loss of their heavy weapons, the Panzer-Divisions in France lost almost everything including at least 20 Flakpanzers

and most of their trucks, guns and equipment. The heaviest losses occurred in August while on the Eastern Front, the greatest losses were in July with almost 1,500 tanks and assault guns lost.

After this, with all the reserves gone, the Panzerwaffe was only a shadow of its former self. In late August, in a desperate move to strengthen its forces, independent Panzer-Brigades began to appear. Most were quickly absorbed into the various Panzer-Divisions, which needed to have their ranks replenished, and sent back into combat. More and more, the Panzer-Divisions were sent back to the front in loosely organized ad hoc groups, often piecemeal. Their armament was mixed which made it difficult to service. As logistical problems increased, many new tanks and assault guns were rendered useless with insufficient fuel and insufficient or incorrect ammunition supplies. In desperation, small units formed from training school officers and men were organized and sent into combat, often paying a high price for their inexperience.

Most Panzer-Divisions continued to fight as a unit until the last days of the war when they destroyed their equipment and surrendered to their enemies. But they were not the same Panzer-Divisions as when they entered WWII. They were certainly better armed but, on the whole, not as well trained. Among the last Panzer-Divisions (in name only) formed, was Panzer-Division 'Clausewitz' which was formed with two battalions of two companies each with a total strength of 56 tanks and assault guns of four different types. Most other divisions were in a similar condition. With names like 'Clausewitz', 'Müncheberg' and 'Schlesien', they were meant to create the impression of strength, but it was paper strength only. At the time of surrender, the combined strength of the Panzerwaffe was 2,023 tanks, 738 assault guns and 159 Flakpanzers - 3,500 vehicles altogether. This was almost the same strength with which they attacked the Soviet Union in 1941. But the situation and the German Army were not the same and the size of the force inadequate for the task. The Panzer-Divisions still existed, but not as the offensive weapon they were in the late 1930's.

I would like to thank the many people who helped me to prepare this 3 volume work with special thanks to Thomas Anderson and Tom Kopanski. All photos used in all three books are taken from various Eastern archives as well as private collections.

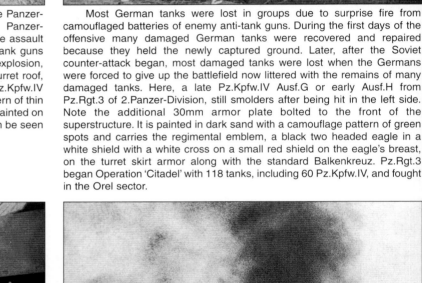

The battle at Kursk ended with heavy losses to almost all the Panzer-Divisions involved. There were instances when the attacking Panzer-Regiment lost up to 40 of its tanks within the first few hours of the assault against well prepared Soviet defenses consisting mostly of anti-tank guns set up in camouflaged firing positions. A catastrophic internal explosion, most likely caused by a large caliber artillery round through the turret roof, has blown the superstructure and turret completely off this Pz.Kpfw.IV Ausf.H. The vehicle is painted in dark sand with a camouflage pattern of thin criss-cross green lines. A small tactical number '624' can be seen painted on the turret schürzen armor, probably in black. In the background can be seen the turretless remains of a Pz.Kpfw.IV Ausf.G.

Most German tanks were lost in groups due to surprise fire from camouflaged batteries of enemy anti-tank guns. During the first days of the offensive many damaged German tanks were recovered and repaired because they held the newly captured ground. Later, after the Soviet counter-attack began, most damaged tanks were lost when the Germans were forced to give up the battlefield now littered with the remains of many damaged tanks. Here, a late Pz.Kpfw.IV Ausf.G or early Ausf.H from Pz.Rgt.3 of 2.Panzer-Division, still smolders after being hit in the left side. Note the additional 30mm armor plate bolted to the front of the superstructure. It is painted in dark sand with a camouflage pattern of green spots and carries the regimental emblem, a black two headed eagle in a white shield with a white cross on a small red shield on the eagle's breast, on the turret skirt armor along with the standard Balkenkreuz. Pz.Rgt.3 began Operation 'Citadel' with 118 tanks, including 60 Pz.Kpfw.IV, and fought in the Orel sector.

Three Pz.Kpfw.IV Ausf.H destroyed by Soviet anti-tank fire - note the two impacts on the rear of the turret of the tank on the left. They are covered with zimmerit, an anti-magnetic mine coating which began to be applied at the factory to most German tanks and assault guns beginning in September 1943. In addition to the standard extra track links placed by the crew in front of the superstructure for extra protection, two T-34 waffle pattern track links can also be seen along the side.

The invincibility of the Tiger I during Operation 'Citadel' is indicated by the number of losses during two months of heavy fighting, no less than 50 vehicles or almost one whole month's production. During the same period, another 16 were lost in Sicily. This Tiger has been set ablaze by the Soviets for propaganda photographs.

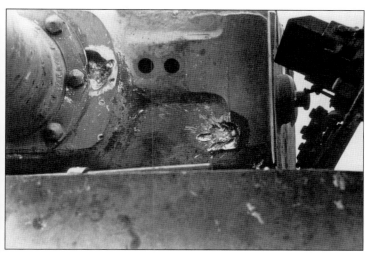

Tiger losses could have been much worse had the Soviets fielded a more potent anti-tank gun than their 76.2mm Field Gun Model 1942. It was also the standard armament of the T-34 medium tank and KV-1 heavy tank and was inadequate against the heavy frontal armor of the Tiger. Here we see traces of two well aimed hits on the mantlet which did not penetrate.

The independent Tiger battalions owed much of their success to their well equipped maintenance companies which kept the vehicles in fighting condition. Large portal cranes such as this were necessary to remove the heavy turret for repairs. The heavy armor of the Tiger made it more resistant to combat damage and after quick repairs, they could be returned to combat to inflict more damage to the enemy. Lighter tanks needed more time for repairs and often had to be transferred to specialized workshops located deep in the rear areas. Tiger 'S12' is from s.SS-Pz.Abt.101 seen in the autumn of 1943.

After removing the turret, it was easy to maintain by the mechanics when placed on the special wooden horses as shown in the foreground or on fuel drums as in the background. Both turrets are fitted with smoke dischargers which were discontinued in June 1943. The style of the turret number '133' indicates these vehicles belong to s.Pz.Abt.503.

Tigers and Pz.Kpfw.III of Panzer-Regiment 'Großdeutschland' hidden in a wood in the Achtyrka sector of Russia, mid August 1943. After the Kursk battle, a new Tiger battalion was formed as III.Abt./Panzer-Regiment 'Großdeutschland' with three companies using the letters 'A', 'B' and 'C' as the first digit in their tactical number. 'B22' seen here, was formerly from 3./s.Pz.Abt.501 which was used to make up the new 10.Kompanie in the regiment.

Mechanics work to replace the Maybach HL230 P45 V12 engine in a Tiger I. The 700 HP motor consumed almost 3 liters of fuel for each kilometer on the road and 5 liters over normal off-road terrain making it one of the less economical vehicles to run in the Panzerwaffe.

A column of Sd.Kfz.250 light armored personnel carriers advance through a Russian village in the southern sector of the Soviet Union during the autumn of 1943. The tactical markings indicate they are from the second company of a motorcycle reconnaissance battalion attached to Panzer-Division 'Großdeutschland'. To the left of the rear access door, a white number '18' indicates this is the 18th vehicle in the company. Unfortunately, the censor has overpainted the vehicle license plate number on this print though the same photo has appeared elsewhere unretouched.

The Germans made extensive use of captured enemy equipment on all fronts during the war. The vehicle in the foreground is a Soviet T-60 light tank that has had its turret removed and is being used as an artillery tractor. In the background is a T34/76 Model 1943 which has a large white outline Balkenkreuz painted on the side of the turret along with a white outline Roman numeral 'II' in front of it. For obvious reasons, they were generally relegated to anti-partisan duties in rear areas.

Soldiers from 'Großdeutschland' load a wounded comrade into an Sd.Kfz.251/1 Ausf.C being utilized temporarily as a Krankenpanzerwagen, or armored ambulance, in early October 1943. It has the standard white outlined Balkenkreuz on its side and an interesting emblem beside the rear door, a stag's head with a cross above it, both painted on a light colored rectangle, similar to the emblem of 521.Pz.Jg.Abt. which was destroyed at Stalingrad.

The main factor in the success of the Panzer-Divisions in Russia was their speed and mobility and the ability to be quickly and efficiently transported from one sector of the front to another by rail transport. Often, when a Panzer-Division was withdrawn from the front, the Soviets would claim it had been annihilated only to be completely surprised to have it appear in another sector several hundred kilometers away. Here, a Pz.Bef.Wg.III Ausf.J, which has been fitted with the wide Winterketten track, is seen loaded onto a railway flatcar along with other divisional vehicles including two Sd.Kfz.251/7 Ausf.D, one of which is missing its bridging sections, for transport to a new battlefield. As the Sd.Kfz.251 Ausf.D version only entered service in September 1943, it is likely that this photograph was taken the following summer.

An Sd.Kfz.7/2 self-propelled anti-aircraft gun on station in October 1943. The mounting of the 3.7cm FlaK36 anti-aircraft gun is clearly shown. Judging from the tent made up of Army splinter pattern Zeltbahn shelter quarters, it is possibly attached to a Wehrmacht Heer unit, although Luftwaffe troops were also issued with the Zeltbahn as well.

Two new vehicles in the Panzerwaffe in the autumn of 1943, were the Schwere Panzerspähwagen (5cm) (Sd.Kfz.234/2) mounting a 5cm KwK39/1, nicknamed the 'Puma', and the Schwere Panzerspähwagen (7.5cm KwK) (Sd.Kfz.234/3) mounting the 7.5cm KwK51 L/24. Here, they are being exhibited on the training ground at Aryss in October 1943 along with other new models of reconnaissance vehicles. The original order for 1,500 Pumas was cut to 100 vehicles in January 1944 in favor of the Sd.Kfz.234/1, mounting the 2cm KwK38 L/55, and Sd.Kfz.234/3, with production terminating in September 1944 after 101 vehicles were produced. Actual production of the Sd.Kfz.234/3 started in June 1944 and continued until December at which time, production of the Sd.Kfz.234/4 mounting the 7.5cm PaK40 L/46 started and continued until the end of the war.

A new Schwimmwagen Typ 166 amphibious car of a Panzer-Division staff traveling through a Russian forest in the autumn of 1943. The black over white over red metal command pennant for a Panzer-Division commander can be seen on the right mudguard. The vehicle is painted in overall dark sand and has a shipping stencil prominently displayed on the side giving the Kfz. number, empty weight, payload weight and vehicle class. The numbers on the side behind the headlight indicate the vehicle type '166' although the significance of the number following is unclear.

A Tiger crewman from s.Pz.Abt.502 pulls on the protective cover over the muzzle brake of his tank during a lull in the action in late 1943. The unit's emblem, a black outline mammoth, can be seen on the front plate next to the machine gun ball mount. Its shape was changed in the spring of 1943 from the earlier version seen in white on the original dark gray vehicles.

An early and a mid-production Tiger I from s.Pz.Abt.502 near Velikye Luki in November 1943. The veteran on the left is still fitted with the smoke candle dischargers on the turret, which were discontinued in June 1943, and has received damage to the commander's cupola hatch, likely from enemy fire. The newer vehicle on the right has the new cupola, a pistol port plug on the rear of the turret just to the left of the soldier's knee and is covered with zimmerit, which was applied starting in September 1943. A white tactical number '1?1' is painted on the side of the turret indicating it is a 1.Kompanie vehicle.

A pair of Pz.Kpfw.IV Ausf.H hidden in a Russian village close to Velikye Luki in autumn 1943. There is no battle damage evident which would indicate they are probably new vehicles. The nearest one is a very early Ausf.H and is still fitted with the additional 30mm armor plates bolted to the front of the upper and lower hull that were introduced on the Ausf.G, while having the newer drive sprocket. Both have turret skirts and support brackets for the side skirts which are not yet installed but often were carried on the vehicle during transport to avoid losing them. Neither has had any camouflage paint applied over the dark sand base, however, the nearest one appears to have a different colored gun barrel.

Two Pz.Kpfw.IV Ausf.H stand by in a field in the Gomel area in November 1943. Nothing remains of the lower hull skirts and brackets on the vehicle in the background. These were often torn off or lost in the heat of battle. To make their life a little more comfortable, the crew have appropriated a couple of chairs which they are carrying on the engine deck, a simple pleasure that most soldiers in the field did without.

A Panzerbefehlswagen III Ausf.K, an Sd.Kfz.251/1 Ausf.C and several Pz.Kpfw.IV Ausf.G in Zhitomir after XXXVIII.Pz.Kp. with 1., 7., 19., 25. and 2.SS-Panzer-Division, recaptured the city in late November 1943. The Befehlspanzer is unusual in that the turret skirts are those of a Pz.Kpfw.IV and not those from a Pz.Kpfw.III as normally used. The battered looking half-track has the tactical number '531' in red with a white outline painted on the side and is missing the shield for the MG34 machine gun.

A new Pz.Kpfw.IV Ausf.G and troops from 1.Panzer-Division occupy Zhitomir in December 1943. The tactical number '842' indicates that this is the second tank in the fourth platoon of the eighth company in the second battalion. It is still painted in its summer camouflage scheme of brown and green over the dark sand base although there does not appear to be much of the base color showing on the turret. In November, the division reported a strength of 95 Pz.Kpfw.IV.

An infantryman, clad in a two piece winter reversible snow suit, confers with officers in an Sd.Kfz.251 Ausf.C half-track during the battles around Zhitomir and Berdichev in late December 1943. The stark white camouflage paint on the half-track contrasts with the surrounding landscape which doesn't appear to have much snow. After the first disastrous winter in Russia, the German Army was better equipped for cold weather combat with a variety of winter uniforms. This one is being worn with the white on the inside and mouse gray on the outside.

Surrendering Soviet troops are taken into captivity by German infantry supported by a StuG.III Ausf.G. It could be from one of the independent Sturmgeschütz Abteilungen or possibly one of the Panzer-Divisions which started to be equipped with these vehicles in their newly created III.Abteilung starting in April 1943. A camouflage scheme of large brown patches has been sprayed over the dark sand base which was common for the early spring and autumn seasons.

The commander of a Pz.Bef.Wg.III Ausf.J receives a communication from a courier in late 1943. 81 vehicles were produced from August to November 1942 with another 104 converted from Pz.Kpfw.III from March to September 1943. This one has been fitted with the early 8 hole drive sprockets with a spacer ring to accommodate the 40cm track. Not visible in the photo is the armored pot mount on the rear of the engine deck for the star antenna. It is finished in a scruffy coat of winter whitewash paint and, unusually, is equipped with the anti-aircraft mount for the MG34. The Roman numeral 'II', painted in black with a white outline, signifies a second battalion staff vehicle.

The German driver of this captured T34/76 Model 1943 smiles for the camera as he emerges from his position during the winter of 1943-44. According to the original press caption, the tank was employed by Panzer-Division 'Großdeutschland'. The Germans put any captured working vehicles to use wherever possible, usually in rear areas where they would not attract unwanted attention from German gunners. The two piece white winter uniform tended to get dirty easily which quickly reduced its camouflage effectiveness.

General Walther Model and some of his staff officers examine a knocked out or captured T34/76 Model 1943 in early 1944. After a short lull in December 1943, heavy fighting resumed in early January and continued until early March 1944, resulting in heavy losses to the Panzer-Divisions. In January alone, 536 tanks, not including self-propelled guns, were lost compared to 596 in July 1943 during the height of the Kursk battle.

The German defenses in the Nevel area in late 1943 were bolstered with about 30 Tigers of s.Pz.Abt.502. Here, one of them, heavily camouflaged with snow covered spruce boughs, guards a road in early January 1944. It is an early vehicle equipped with S-mine dischargers on the hull, an early cupola and lacks zimmerit. The tank has an interesting camouflage pattern of brown patches applied over the dark sand base and a white tactical number '101' painted on the turret, indicating it is a first company command vehicle.

Tigers of s.Pz.Abt.502 attack with German infantry support during the heavy fighting around Nevel in late December 1943 and early January 1944. At the end of December, the first company was sent by train to the Leningrad sector, leaving the other two companies to continue the battle. Their powerful guns and strong armor turned back several Soviet assaults that threatened to break the German lines.

In early January 1944, the battle continued in the Nevel area and fighting renewed in the Narva-Leningrad area where H.Gr.Nord fought to contain strong Soviet offensives aimed at lifting the siege of Leningrad. Here, two Pz.Kpfw.IV Ausf.H are advancing across a snow covered field somewhere on the Eastern Front during that winter. They are both camouflaged with a dirty coat of winter whitewash and carry three digit stenciled white outline tactical numbers on the side of the turret schürzen, the closest one being '312' and the far one '221'.

A column of Tigers from s.Pz.Abt.505 south of Vitebsk in the middle of February, 1944. The battalion played a major part in the defensive actions in the central sector of the Eastern Front, supporting the infantry divisions as a fire brigade. Employed in the Vitebsk area with 3.Panzer-Armee since late 1943, the battalion lost about 25% of its strength in six weeks and by the middle of February, only 18 Tigers were on inventory.

The original press caption for this Sd.Kfz.251 indicates that it is an ambulance, but this is unlikely as it is obviously armed with an MG34 machine gun. The curved rail that was normally fitted in front of the shield is missing leaving the mounting strip in place. Behind the grenadier, the folded canvas cover and the curved front support hoop can be seen.

A mid production Tiger I hidden at the edge of a Russian forest in January/February 1944. It probably belonged to s.Pz.Abt.506 which marked their tanks with large one and two digit tactical markings, although they were usually on the front half of the turret, not on the rear as this '1' is. The Tiger carries zimmerit which has been covered with white winter camouflage paint along with a small Balkenkreuz on the side of the hull in a patch of the dark sand base color.

In late January 1944, Oberstleutnant Dr. Franz Bake, commander of Pz.Rgt.11 of 6.Panzer-Division, was given the task of spearheading the attack attempting to relieve the Korsun-Cherkassy Pocket, where about 56,000 German troops were trapped. In addition to his regiment, he was placed in command of s.Pz.Abt.503 with 34 Tigers and II./Pz.Rgt.23 with 47 Pz.Kpfw.V Panther. The new unit was to be named s.Pz.Rgt. Bake. Here we see one of the Tigers and an early Pz.Kpfw.V Panther Ausf.A as the unit makes ready for battle.

Two photographs of vehicles abandoned by 1.Panzer-Armee on the road leading out of the Korsun-Cherkassy Pocket after the breakout attempt. The two early Pz.Kpfw.V Panther Ausf.A, a few Maultiers and a StuG.III Ausf.G of 5.SS-Panzer-Division 'Wiking' are shown here in March 1944. It appears that these vehicles were destroyed by their crews after running out of fuel as evidenced by the internal explosion that blew off the turret roof of the Panther. The still connected tow cables indicate it had been immobilized.

Two Pz.Kpfw.IV Ausf.H and an Sd.Kfz.251 half-track accompanied by infantry make their way across the frozen wasteland of the Eastern Front in the winter of 1943-44. The tank appears to be new as all of its schürzen are intact and there is no apparent damage. It has a uniform coat of white winter camouflage paint and a three digit tactical number '821' in a black stencil outline with a Balkenkreuz in front of it.

A column of infantry laden Pz.Kpfw.IV Ausf.H, possibly from II./Pz.Rgt.11 of s.Pz.Rgt.Bake, near the village of Pogrebishtche in February 1944. In order to maintain their speed, the accompanying infantry were carried on the tanks and trucks into the battle. When they ran into stiff opposition, they would dismount to protect themselves from heavy losses. Though the tanks have white winter camouflage paint applied, most has been worn off, thereby limiting its effectiveness.

A 'Wespe' self-propelled gun armed with a 10.5cm lFH18M howitzer sits in firing position on the Eastern Front near the village of Pogrebishtche in February 1944 while the crew prepare foxholes for themselves. The upper hull has been painted in a uniform coat of white winter camouflage paint while the lower hull is covered with snow buildup, some of which has fallen off revealing the dark gray base coat. The only visible marking is a black outline Balkenkreuz on the side of the fighting compartment.

A trio of Tigers from s.Pz.Abt.503 abandoned somewhere in Russia, probably late 1943. This particular vehicle has been previously photographed while fitted with a Pz.Kpfw.III stowage bin on the rear of the turret and is readily identifiable by the slightly crooked manner in which the turret numbers have been applied. The tactical number and Balkenkreuz are both black with a white outline.

A 'Nashorn' self-propelled anti-tank gun, mounting the deadly 8.8cm PaK43/1 L/71, fires at an enemy target during one of the Eastern Front battles in the winter of 1943-44. In addition to its white winter camouflage paint, the vehicle carries the name 'Tiger' on the side along with a white outlined Balkenkreuz, also repeated on the left rear. A large unit emblem in the shape of a shield can be seen just behind the open right rear access door but, unfortunately, is not clear enough to be identified. The 'Nashorn' was introduced in time for the battle at Kursk in July 1943 and proved to be a highly effective tank killer until replaced in 1944 by the Jadgpanzer IV and Jagdpanther.

A battery of 'Hummel' self-propelled guns mounting the 15cm sFH18 howitzer prepare to fire at enemy targets in February-March 1944. The chassis of the 'Hummel' was identical to that used for the 'Nashorn'. White winter camouflage paint has been applied uniformly to one of the vehicles while the other two have an irregular pattern leaving some of their base color showing through. As usual, the only markings visible are the white outline black national crosses on the sides.

A new 'Hummel' self-propelled gun, probably from I./Pz.Art.Rgt.73 of 1.Panzer-Division, sits in position near Tarnopol in the spring of 1944. It is painted in dark sand with the chassis number '320264' painted in white on the front of the fighting compartment. The frame mounted on the hull in front of the driver was to aid him in lining the vehicle up in its firing position.

A late StuG.III Ausf.G advances through a burning village near Vitebsk in March 1944. It is fitted with the 'topfblende' cast gun mantlet and shot deflector in front of the cupola that were installed on Sturmgeschütz produced starting in the fall of 1943. Since the spring of 1943, Sturmgeschütz were used to create a new III.Abteilung in some of the Panzer-Divisions to increase their operational strength due to low production rates for the more expensive standard gun tanks.

Two Pz.Kpfw.IV Ausf.H fire from a hull down position while the Sd.Kfz.250 on the right sits safely below the crest of the hill in early April 1944. April was a costly month for the Panzerwaffe in the east when 700 tanks, not including self-propelled guns, were lost. Most of these were counted in 1.Panzer-Armee in the Ukraine where they were forced to battle their way through Soviet encirclements at Korsun-Cherkassy and then Kamenets-Podolsk.

German infantry help clear a path through the deep snow to provide passage for a column of Pz.Kpfw.IV Ausf.H from an unidentified Panzer-Division in March 1944. Deep snow had the same effect as mud on an armored vehicle. If the vehicle bottomed out, the tracks would spin freely immobilizing it. On the leading tank, a Balkenkreuz with a white outline can be seen on the turret schürzen followed by a tactical number beginning with a '2'.

Tigers from s.Pz.Abt.506 cross a shallow stream in the Ukraine in May 1944. The colorful emblem of this unit, a large 'W' with a shield and a tiger, can be clearly seen on the rear of the turret stowage bin. The 'W' stood for the battalion's first commander, Major Willing, who was killed in action on October 23, 1943. On staff vehicles, the 'W' was green while on 1.Kompanie vehicles it was white, with 2.Kompanie being red and 3.Kompanie yellow. The shields were all red with a white cross and the tigers all yellow. This then, is a Tiger from 1.Kompanie.

A pair of Sd.Kfz.251/1 Ausf.D half-tracks support the advance of Tigers from s.Pz.Abt.507 in the Tarnopol area in April 1944. The Tiger is a late production vehicle fitted with steel roadwheels and displays the unusual style of tactical numbering used by this battalion. The large company number is followed by smaller platoon and vehicle numbers, in this case '213', in white with a thin black outline.

A Tiger I of s.Pz.Abt.507 near Tarnopol after the relief of the city in mid April 1944. They were supported in the attempt by elements of 9.SS-Panzer-Division 'Hohenstauffen' and a small battlegroup formed from various other units, advancing to within seven miles of the city and allowing a small contingent to break out.

A column of Pz.Kpfw.V Panther Ausf.A from Panzer-Regiment 'Großdeutschland' and other divisional soft-skin vehicles on a road near Jassy, Romania in early April 1944. Most of the snow has disappeared but the ground is still firmly frozen as can be seen by the condition of the dirt road these vehicles are traveling on. These are early production Ausf.A fitted with the new cast cupola but still retaining the MG flap in the glacis.

A battery of 'Hummel' self-propelled guns sit in position somewhere in Romania in early May 1944. An attempt has been made to camouflage the vehicles with branches so their winter camouflage schemes will not be so noticeable on the spring landscape. The paint was usually thinned with water which made it easy to wash off when it was no longer necessary.

When spring thaw occurred, the primitive dirt roads in eastern Europe turned to an almost impassable bog. Here, a column of 'Hummel' self-propelled guns struggle along a dirt road flanked on both sides by water filled ditches. Remnants of their winter camouflage schemes can still be seen.

A Pz.Kpfw.IV Ausf.H of 4.Panzer-Division camouflaged with branches, guards a German trench in the Kovel area in April-May 1944. The new divisional emblem can be seen just behind the white, three digit tactical number, '611', painted on the turret schürzen. In front of that is the original divisional emblem, a standing bear, probably painted in red with a white outline. The new emblem, a black shield containing the original tactical sign of the division, over crossed swords, was adopted in early 1944 to honor the divisional commander's award of the Swords to the Knights Cross. The emblem was enlarged on the division's Pz.Kpfw.IV to include 'I./Pz.Rgt.35' and the rhomboid tactical sign for a Panzer-Division followed by a subscript number indicating the company to which the vehicle belonged, all painted in yellow.

A Pz.Kpfw.IV Ausf.H fords a small river somewhere in the Ukraine in May 1944. Despite the spring weather, the tank still carries its white winter camouflage paint causing it to stand out against the new growth. A white outlined Balkenkreuz can be seen on the turret schürzen followed by the first digit in its tactical number, an '8', probably in yellow with a black outline.

An old Pz.Kpfw.V Panther Ausf.D still in service on the Eastern Front in the late spring of 1944. The last of the Ausf.D production were built in August 1943 at which time the new Ausf.A made its appearance. The first Ausf.A, while fitted with the new commander's cupola, still retained the MG flap on the glacis.

A group of NCO's on leave, visit an NSKK center where members of the 'Hitlerjugend' receive instruction on the operation of motorcycles in early March 1944. The Knights Cross winner in the background is Oberwachtmeister Willi Kessel who served in 3.Kompanie of Panzer-Aufklärung-Abteilung 'Großdeutschland' as a platoon commander. He was awarded the Knights Cross on February 23, 1944 for an action on October 23, 1943, during which he led a small force, capturing a hill overlooking the Dniepr River and, despite being wounded, held the position until relieved.

These three photographs graphically demonstrate the effect of dwindling oil reserves on Germany's conduct of the war. Approximately 180,000 civilian and military vehicles were converted to use gas-generators that burned a variety of solid fuels, primarily dried wood, charcoal, anthracite, low temperature coke and peat. In the right photo, we see an Opel Blitz which appears to be having its solid fuel supply replenished. In the top photo, two SS soldiers hurriedly exit from an Organization Todt lorrie carrying the vehicle license number 'OT-15838'. The bottom photo is a captured U.S. manufactured 1937 Chevrolet being used by the German Navy as indicated by the 'WM' license number plate mounted in front.

A new Tiger I sits on a railway flatcar on its way to Panzer-Division 'Großdeutschland' in May 1944. There are no visible markings but the distinctive cuffband of the division can be seen on some of the crew uniforms. The vehicle has been prepared for rail transport following standard procedures with the narrow transport tracks installed, the side mudguards removed and the turret traversed to the rear with the gun barrel securely blocked with a wooden cradle. The wide battle tracks can be seen stowed underneath the vehicle.

An interesting photograph of three rare Tigers on the Eastern Front during the summer of 1944. The Tiger in the middle has the chassis number '250287' stenciled on the front which indicates it is one of 60 produced in June 1943 but it is covered with zimmerit which was not applied until starting in September 1943. The vehicle on the left is a Panzerbefehlswagen Tiger, identifiable by the antenna mounted on the left side of the engine deck, also fitted with the early cupola and having zimmerit. On the right is an even earlier production vehicle which does not have the spare track link brackets on the turret that were introduced in April 1943. It is also covered with zimmerit as well. All three have white tactical numbers on the turrets outlined with black. In August 1943, s.Pz.Abt.506 reported receiving 45 new Tigers, all with zimmerit, three of which still had the early cupola. This may well be those three vehicles.

A late production Tiger I of s.Pz.Abt.507 passing through a burning village somewhere near the Polish-Russian border in the early summer of 1944. During the fighting withdrawal conducted after the launch of Operation 'Bagration', the Soviet summer offensive, the battalion lost 13, almost one third, of its Tigers in the first three weeks of August. The identifying large first digit of the tactical number can be faintly seen on the side of the turret. Large bundles of fascines have been fastened to each side of the hull.

A column of new Pz.Kpfw.IV Ausf.H march toward the front, possibly in East Prussia, during the summer of 1944. They are heavily camouflaged with foliage as protection against Soviet fighters, which by that time, controlled the skies. It is painted in a standard three color camouflage scheme of green and brown patches over the dark sand base with markings limited to a white outlined Balkenkreuz painted on the side of the turret schürzen. A pair of spare roadwheels is propped against the front plate along with a pair on which the rubber tires are missing.

The crew of this Pz.Kpfw.IV Ausf.H enjoy a cigarette break in France during the summer of 1944. The vehicle is fitted with the newer drive sprocket and all steel return rollers which were introduced in the previous year along with a single 80mm front plate and zimmerit anti-magnetic mine coating.

Command version of the Sd.Kfz.234/2 Puma equipped with additional radios and a star antenna mounted on the engine deck, most likely in France during the summer of 1944. The vehicle is painted in a three color camouflage scheme of green and brown over the dark sand base and has heavy foliage cover as well. On the turret, a tactical number, '023' or '025', is painted in black with a white outline. Of special interest is the very light color of the muzzle brake on the 5cm main armament.

Another photo of a command Puma racing down a road on the Eastern Front in June 1944. It is finished in dark sand without any camouflage paint and has no markings other than the vehicle license number 'WH-1618820'. With only 101 manufactured, it was a rarely photographed vehicle.

Two 'Panther' Ausf.G advance down a country road in northern France during the summer of 1944. Due to the lighting, it is difficult to discern whether or not they have had any camouflage paint applied, but it is almost certain they would have. The first one is covered with foliage to help it blend in with the countryside as Allied airpower was the most dangerous opponent faced by German tanks on the Western Front. On the second vehicle, little remains of the foliage, but some is still evident. The tactical number '411' can be faintly seen on the side of the turret.

A 'Panther' Ausf.A from 3.SS-Panzer-Division 'Totenkopf' in action in the summer of 1944, probably in the Kovel area. The zimmerit pattern is plainly visible on the glacis and schürzen but the turret appears to have none on the sides. The white tactical number '714' indicates that this 'Panther' is from the seventh company in the second battalion. Just to the left of the MG ball mount, the division's 'totenkopf' insignia can be seen painted in white.

A Pz.Kpfw.V Panther Ausf.G swings off the road and through a hedgerow in France, June 1944. Unusually, the vehicle has no camouflage paint applied over its dark sand base. The rather large tactical number '421' appears to be newly painted in black with a white outline. As well, a white outline Balkenkreuz can also be seen on the rear of the hull between the exhaust pipes, partially obscured by the jack.

The commander of a Pz.Kpfw.IV Ausf.J receives orders from an Sd.Kfz.251/3 Ausf.C command half-track somewhere on the Eastern Front in early autumn 1944. An identifying feature of the Ausf.J is the lack of a muffler for the auxiliary turret traverse motor beside the engine muffler and the square cover on the engine deck over the radiator filler caps. Additionally, the vehicle does not have the zimmerit coating that was eliminated beginning in September 1944. The tactical number '521' is painted in red with a white outline beside a white outlined Balkenkreuz. The tactical number '2101' on the half-track is painted in black with a white outline.

The summer of 1944 was a bitter struggle for the German Panzertruppe on the Eastern Front which resulted in severe losses in all the units involved. Among them was this Pz.Kpfw.IV Ausf.G with a white stenciled outline tactical number '332' appearing on the side of the turret which would indicate the tank was refitted with the schürzen armor on the turret and hull in a field workshop. The white elephant emblem on the rear of the turret schürzen beside the tactical number is that of s.Pz.Abt.502. This is one of at least two Pz.Kpfw.IV Ausf.G used by the battalion, though none appear on any known strength reports.

A column of Pz.Kpfw.V Panther Ausf.G, carrying infantry, on the march in France, late summer 1944. They are camouflaged with branches and hug the sides of the road to avoid detection from Allied fighters. The first two Ausf.G were built by M.A.N. in March 1944 and they began to be distributed to the Panzer-Divisions in April when a total of 105 were completed. Production of the Ausf.A continued at the MNH plant until July when they converted over to Ausf.G.

Two heavily camouflaged Pz.Kpfw.V Panther Ausf.G in a Norman village in July 1944. They are possibly from Panzer-Lehr-Division which was in the Normandy area when the invasion began. On June 10, 1944, they reported a strength of 98 Pz.Kpfw.IV and 88 Panthers. By July 8, 41 Pz.Kpfw.IV and 36 Panthers were reported as total losses.

A Flakpanzerkampfwagen IV (3.7cm FlaK43) (Sd.Kfz.161/3) self-propelled anti-aircraft gun, known as the 'Möbelwagen', from the same unit. The first 20 'Möbelwagen' were completed by the end of March 1944 and began to be issued to the Panzer-Divisions on June 15, 1944, with eight going to each of the 9., 11., and 116.Panzer-Divisions in Normandy. A further sixteen were issued to 6. and 19.Panzer-Division on the Eastern Front. Four each were issued to Panzer-Brigade 105, 106, 107 and 108 on the Western Front and another four to each of the other six Panzer-Brigades on the Eastern Front. Starting in September 1944, Panzer-Regiments and Abteilungen as well as Panzer-Jäger-Abteilung began to be issued with four 'Möbelwagen' and four 'Wirbelwind'.

Pz.Kpfw.IV Ausf.H, Pz.Rgt.1, 1.Panzer-Division, Zhitomir, December 1943

This late model Pz.Kpfw.IV Ausf.G is painted in overall dark sand and has a camouflage scheme of large green patches and smaller brown ones. Very little of the dark sand base is visible on the turret schürzen. The tactical number, '842', is painted in white on the forward turret schürzen access door and also on the rear of the schürzen. As most Ausf.G were fitted in the field with schürzen, the original placement of the standard white outline Balkenkreuz on the hull sides still remained.

Sd.Kfz.165 'Hummel', unknown Pz.Art.Rgt., Eastern Front, February-March 1944

This early production 'Hummel' is painted in overall dark sand and has a white winter camouflage paint scheme applied in an irregular, hard edge pattern leaving only the white outline Balkenkreuz visible.

Pz.Bef.Wg.III Ausf.J, unknown Panzer-Division, Russia, summer 1944

This Pz.Bef.Wg.III Ausf.J is identifiable by the antenna pot on the rear of the engine deck and additional antenna swivel mount on the left hull side, just in front of the air intake housing. It is painted in overall dark sand and has a camouflage scheme of thin green and brown wavy lines. Markings appear to be limited to the white outline Balkenkreuz on the side of the turret schürzen, although there may have been other markings on the missing rear part of the skirt armor. This vehicle was also fitted with the wide winterketten tracks.

Pz.Bef.Wg.V 'Panther' Ausf.G, Pz.Rgt.15, 11.Panzer-Division, southern France, summer 1944

This Pz.Bef.Wg.V 'Panther' Ausf.G is painted in overall dark sand and has no camouflage paint scheme. The panther head emblem on the side of the turret was first used by Pz.Abt.52 at Kursk before they were incorporated into Pz.Rgt.15 of 11.Panzer-Division on August 24, 1943. This is followed by a standard white outline Balkenkreuz and a tactical number 'IN3', painted in red with a thin white outline and indicates it is a Nachrichten staff vehicle with I.Bataillon.

Pz.Kpfw. Tiger Ausf.B, 3./s.Pz.Abt.503, Mailly-le-Camp, France, July 1944

3./s.Pz.Abt.503 was equipped with 14 new Tiger II with the early turret, some of which still had the monobloc 8.8cm KwK43 L/71 gun barrel. This Tiger II has a camouflage scheme of large patches of green and brown, leaving little of the dark sand base color showing. The tactical number, '334', is painted in red with a white outline and the Balkenkreuz has a small circle of the dark sand color surrounding it.

Sd.Kfz.234/2 'Puma', unknown Pz.Aufkl.Abt., France, summer 1944

This 'Puma' eight wheeled armored car has a camouflage paint scheme of brown and green patches over the overall dark sand base and s covered with a heavy layer of foliage to help it blend in with its surroundings. A three digit tactical number, '023' or '025', painted in black with a white outline, can be seen on the side of the turret, partially concealed by the foliage. The muzzle brake is an unusually light color.

Sd.Kfz.233, unknown Pz.Aufkl.Abt., Poland, summer 1944
This is a later production vehicle that has raised sides on the superstructure around the fighting compartment. The crew have also added an additional spaced armor plate on the front. It is painted in overall dark sand with a random application of green and brown camouflage in wavy lines. There are no visible markings.

Pz.Kpfw.VI Tiger I Ausf.E., 1./s.Pz.Abt.506, Poland, August 1944
This mid-production Tiger I has a camouflage scheme of brown patches over the dark sand base. The large single digit tactical number, '6', painted in white, indicates this is a 1.Kompanie vehicle. The only other markings on this unit's Tigers, was the colorful emblem painted on the rear of the turret stowage bin, with the color of the 'W' matching the company color. On staff vehicles, the color was green.

Opel Blitz with 2cm FlaK38, unknown Wehrmacht FlaK unit, Russia, summer 1944
This Opel Blitz 3-ton truck has an elaborate camouflage scheme of green and brown lines and patches applied over the dark sand base. No markings other than the standard vehicle license plates are carried.

Pz.Kpfw.IV Ausf.J, 2111.Pz.Abt., 111.Pz.Brig., eastern France, September 1944
This Pz.Kpfw.IV Ausf.J is painted with a camouflage scheme of large green vertical stripes applied over the dark sand base. Markings include a three digit tactical number and Balkenkreuz painted on the turret schürzen sides and back, here obscured by the heavy foliage covering the vehicle. Additionally, a small 'vB' is painted in white on the hinged portion of the left front mudguard, probably signifying the name of the unit commander, von Bronsart.

Flakpanzer IV 'Wirbelwind', unknown FlaK.Art.Abt., France, summer 1944

This 'Wirbelwind' was built on the chassis of a Pz.Kpfw.IV Ausf.G and is painted in overall dark sand with a camouflage scheme of green patches applied over the vehicle and turret. As unusual on the Western Front in 1944, foliage liberally covers the vehicle to break up the shape and blend it in with its surroundings.

Pz.Kpfw.V 'Panther' Ausf.G, unknown Panzer-Division, Germany, January 1945

This late model 'Panther' Ausf.G is fitted with the chin style mantlet and raised fan cover for the crew compartment heater. It has a very striking winter camouflage scheme of wide white lines applied over the summer camouflage in a zig-zag fashion on the turret and hull sides and also on the roadwheels. The only visible marking is the standard Balkenkreuz which is painted on the hull side in an unusual location.

Pz.IV/70 (A) 'Zwischenlösung', unknown Panzer-Division, Czechoslovakia, spring 1945

This vehicle is painted in overall dark sand with an ambush camouflage scheme of green and brown patches. A standard Balkenkreuz has been painted below the top of the fighting compartment near the middle and a three digit tactical number, '611', is painted in a white outline near the front. Unusually, this vehicle has only three steel wheels on the front two bogies instead of the normal four.

StuG.III Ausf.G, unknown StuG.Abt., Czechoslovakia, spring 1945

This StuG.III Ausf.G is fitted with a very unique schürzen arrangement that gives it a strong resemblance to the Jagdpanzer IV, as well as an additional, larger MG shield placed in front of the original one. The vehicle was carefully repainted with dark sand and a camouflage scheme of large brown patches. On the upper side plates, a Balkenkreuz appears, while a two or three digit tactical number beginning with '12' or '13' (on the original print, a civilian is standing in front of the vehicle and is blocking the view) is painted in red or black with a white outline on the lower plate.

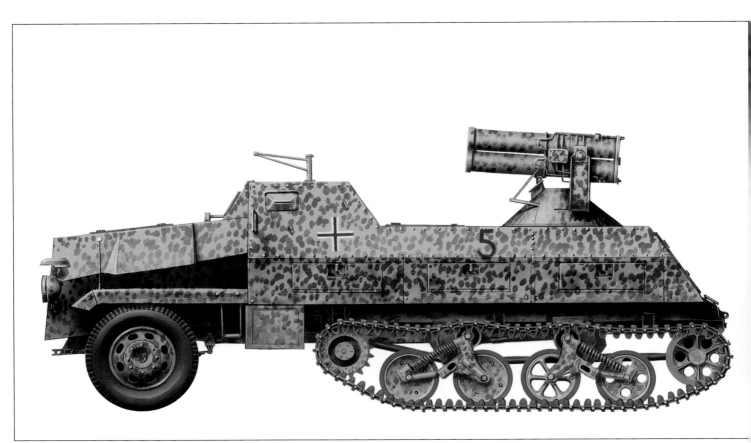

Sd.Kfz.4/1 Panzerwerfer 42, unknown Panzer-Division, Eastern Front, spring 1945

This Panzerwerfer 42 is painted in overall dark sand with a green and brown camouflage pattern applied in small spots over the entire vehicle including the running gear. A thin style Balkenkreuz and a black tactical number '5' are painted on the side.

Sd.Kfz.251/9 Ausf.D, Panzer-Division 'Großdeutschland', East Prussia, 1945

This armored half-track has an unusual winter camouflage consisting of white wavy lines on the hull side extensions and front while the rest of the vehicle has been uniformly covered. A large three digit tactical number, '427', is painted in white on the side. Some effort has been taken to leave a thin outline of the base color exposed around each number when the winter camouflage was applied.

An infantry machine gun squad dismounts from a Pz.Kpfw.V Panther Ausf.G somewhere in Poland during the late summer of 1944. The Panther appears to be fairly new and has zimmerit coating. In early September, zimmerit was dropped along with the requirement to paint the vehicles with dark sand paint. The assembly plants were ordered to apply light patches of camouflage paint directly over the vehicle leaving much of the red oxide primer exposed.

Oberst Willi Langkeit, second from the left with Knights Cross and commander of Pz.Rgt. 'Großdeutschland', relaxes in front of his personal Pz.Bef.Wg.V Panther Ausf.A in June 1944. The tactical number '01', painted in black, changed from the month before when it was simply '0' when photographed at Targul Frumos. As well, it displays a new camouflage paint scheme not seen previously. Also note the small black 'stahlhelm' emblem of the division painted beside the number.

41

A pair of new Pz.Bef.Wg.V Panther Ausf.G, possibly from Pz.Rgt.15 of 11.Panzer-Division, in southern France during the summer of 1944. On the side of the turret, just in front of the national cross, is a black panther head emblem similar to that used by Pz.Abt.52 at Kursk in 1943. On August 24, 1943, Pz.Abt.52 was renamed I./Pz.Rgt.15. In June 1944, the remnants of the division which had been decimated on the Eastern Front, were sent to Bordeaux in southern France and refitted. In July, they were transported east to Toulouse and in August took part in the action against the Allied landings in southern France. The tactical number, 'IN3', painted in red with a thin white outline, indicates it is a Nachrichten staff vehicle in the first battalion. The tactical number on the second vehicle is 'IN1'. Other views of these vehicles appear on page 52 of 'Panzerwaffe at War (2) Moscow to Berlin'.

A Pz.Kpfw.V Panther Ausf.G and a rarely photographed late Pz.Kpfw.IV Ausf.J in a village in eastern France in the autumn of 1944. There are many interesting features on the Pz.Kpfw.IV including the 'Flammentoeter' mufflers introduced in August, the wire mesh schürzen introduced in September and the pivoting commander's cupola hatch introduced in October 1944. In addition, it has a very uncommon 'ambush' camouflage paint scheme. Note as well, the three digit tactical number '615' in red with a white outline painted over the Balkenkreuz. Both vehicles have scraps of wood from damaged houses placed around to make them more difficult to spot from the air.

Two photographs of a Pz.Bef.Wg.V Panther Ausf.G from an Army Panzer-Division. It has several rows of spare track links hanging from the side of the turret to bolster its armor protection which was common during the later stages of the war. The white outline tactical number 'IIA1' indicate it is a staff vehicle in second battalion.

A column of Pz.Kpfw.V Panther and transport vehicles of all types on the retreat somewhere on the Eastern Front, summer 1944. The closest one is an Ausf.A and is fitted with the twin cooling pipes on the left side exhaust that were introduced in January 1944. Mud thrown up on the rear of the stowage bin has almost obscured the Balkenkreuz painted there.

A Pz.Kpfw.V Panther Ausf.G emerges from a forest track during the summer of 1944 in France. During the day, it was critical to make the best possible use of the natural terrain for cover against Allied air power. In July and August alone, 663 Panthers were lost in all theaters of operation.

A similar situation in another sector on the Eastern Front. Here, a long column of Pz.Kpfw.IV Ausf.H advance past a column of transport trucks, some towing trailers, heading in the opposite direction. The leading vehicle has a white three digit tactical number '609' painted on the turret schürzen behind the standard Balkenkreuz. The crew have placed a salvaged piece of hull schürzen on the turret roof as additional protection from air attack. Another example of this practice can be seen on page 71 in 'Panzertruppen at War' where a Pz.Kpfw.V Panther Ausf.G has been similarly modified.

A veteran of the battles of the previous year, this early Tiger I is from s.Pz.Abt.502, seen in the summer of 1944. By this time, the battalion had changed the style of tactical numbering to red with a white outline. As the battalion was overstrength, there were 9 vehicles in the staff and first platoons of each company, which would explain the high tactical number '307'. Note that the first outside roadwheel is missing. They were commonly removed by the crews as mud tended to build up and clog the drive sprockets.

Another Tiger I of s.Pz.Abt.502 having its ammunition replenished while the activity is recorded by a Kriegsberichter who can be seen standing on the front of the vehicle. The tactical number '210' is also painted in red with a white outline. This vehicle is one of those built between October and December 1943 with the gun travel lock mounted on the rear of the hull. It is also missing the front outside roadwheel.

A battle worn Pz.Kpfw.IV Ausf.J in France, late summer 1944. A three digit tactical number starting with a '6' and ending with a '4' can be seen on the rear of the turret schürzen and is probably red with a white outline. The turret traverse motor was dropped in February 1944 and along with it, the small muffler that was mounted to the left of the main exhaust muffler.

A Pz.Kpfw.V Panther Ausf.A, probably from the same unit, followed close behind by a staff car. The pattern in the zimmerit coating can be plainly seen and it appears that no camouflage paint or markings applied.

A Pz.Kpfw.V Panther Ausf.G kicks up a cloud of dust as it travels down a country road in France in early September 1944. The markings on the turret side are too faint to identify but of special interest is the unusual white triangle painted on the rear turret hatch, the significance of which is unknown.

Another new vehicle to the Panzerwaffe in 1944 was the Flakpanzerkampfwagen IV (2cm Flakvierling 38) (Sd.Kfz.161/4) self-propelled anti-aircraft gun, known as the 'Wirbelwind'. These were assembled on rebuilt Pz.Kpfw.IV chassis that had been returned to Germany. This one is based on a Pz.Kpfw.IV Ausf.G identifiable by the 30mm armor plates welded to the front of the hull and superstructure. The first 17 were completed in July 1944 and, starting in September, began to be issued to the various units on the basis of four 'Wirbelwind' and four 'Möbelwagen' each.

Two Flakpanzer IV 'Wirbelwind' photographed in early October somewhere on the Western Front. They have also been built on Pz.Kpfw.IV Ausf.G chassis and have standard three color camouflage paint schemes consisting of green and brown patches on the dark sand base. As usual, they have been liberally covered with branches to improve their camouflage. A total of 122 vehicles were completed by the end of March 1945.

Three photos of a Pz.Kpfw.IV Ausf.J from 2111.Panzer-Abteilung, 111.Panzer-Brigade, in the Lorraine area of France, September 1944. This short-lived brigade, made up of Pz.Abt.2111, equipped with 10 StuG.III, 45 Pz.Kpfw.IV and 8 Flakpanzer IV and I./Pz.Rgt.16 with 45 Pz.Kpfw.V Panther, was formed on September 4, 1944 and disbanded and integrated into 11.Panzer-Division on October 1, 1944. A tactical number, '838', is painted in black beside the Balkenkreuz on one of the vehicles. The inscription, 'vB', on the mudguard of the other, may stand for 'von Bronsart', the unit commander.

The German Army left the demolished remains of its once vaunted Panzer-Divisions all across the European continent in the summer of 1944. This Pz.Kpfw.V Panther Ausf.A was knocked out by Polish or Canadian forces near Falaise in August 1944. A group of Commonwealth pilots pose with 'their kill' for the benefit of the folks back home. Although fighters took a terrible toll of German armor, it is just as likely that this Panther was destroyed by ground forces.

Two Pz.Kpfw.V Panther Ausf.G of 19.Panzer-Division, knocked out by Polish or Soviet forces in the Studzianki area. A fire has ravaged the first vehicle, burning off the rubber tires on the roadwheels. The fire weakened torsion bar suspension has collapsed lowering it noticeably to the ground. The other vehicle also appears to have some fire damage as well. The chassis number, '120734', can still be seen painted in black on the glacis, indicating that it was built in July 1944 at the M.A.N. assembly plant. 19.Panzer-Division was transferred back to Germany from the Eastern Front in May 1944 and was refitted as a 'Panzer-Division 44' in Holland in July/August 1944, with one battalion of Pz.Kpfw.V and one of Pz.Kpfw.IV. They were immediately sent back into action in Poland.

The crew of a Pz.Kpfw.IV struggles to repair a damaged track. This was a difficult job at the best of times and in action, was much more difficult and dangerous. Often, minor damage such as this resulted in the complete loss of the vehicle if repairs were impossible to carry out because of combat conditions.

This series of five photographs shows a meeting up of two Wehrmacht reconnaissance troops in a field somewhere north-east of Warsaw in August/September 1944. One is equipped with several Sd.Kfz.222, Schwimmwagen and an Sd.Kfz.261 mounting a frame antenna. A close look at the Sd.Kfz.222 turret would seem to indicate the armored cars are in their original dark gray paint with a dark sand camouflage pattern. The other unit is equipped with Sd.Kfz.233 heavy armored cars, equipped with the 7.5cm StuK37 L/24 gun and raised superstructures around the fighting compartment. They are most likely painted in dark sand with a two color, wavy camouflage pattern. Both vehicles have been fitted with a field modified additional armor plate on the front.

A pair of Jagdpanzer 38(t) 'Hetzer' tank destroyers used by the Germans against the Polish underground army in Warsaw at the beginning of August 1944. Production of these vehicles started in April 1944 and by July 1944, the first combat units began to receive them. They are painted in dark sand with a two color camouflage scheme of green patches with a dark brown outline, best seen on the lead vehicle in the background.

Two photographs of a 'Hetzer' that has been captured by the Poles and is being used in a street barricade in Warsaw, September 1944. The Poles captured three of these vehicles in August and September, one of which was repaired and used against the Germans. This is one of the early models as indicated by the shape of the mantlet. It is also missing the roof and may have suffered an internal explosion. The camouflage scheme is similar to the other two in the photo above .

A Borgward B IV Ausf.C (Sd.Kfz.301) demolition vehicle from Pz.Abt. (FKL) 302 sits abandoned on a Warsaw street in August/September 1944, where they were used extensively against Polish partisans hidden in buildings and behind barricades. The Borgwards were radio controlled from a command vehicle, in this case a StuG.III Ausf.G, which guided them to their target where a 500kg explosive charge was dropped. The Borgward was then backed away a safe distance and the charge detonated. On this one, the charge is missing. A camouflage paint scheme can be made out along with the load class shipping stencil on the side.

This StuG.III Ausf.G, also abandoned on a Warsaw street, may have been one of the command vehicles from Pz.Abt. (FKL) 302 or Sturmgeschütz-Ersatz-Abteilung 200, the only two Sturmgeschütz units employed in this bloody battle except for a few used by the Kaminski RONA or Dirlewanger Brigades.

Elements from one of the Panzer-Divisions cross the Duna River during the retreat from Lithuania and Belorussia around August 20, 1944. Despite Soviet air superiority, the Germans were able to make the crossing without much interference. Among the vehicles being ferried over are an Opel Blitz, an ambulance and two staff cars in the left photo and two Sd.Kfz.10's in the right photo.

A battery of 8.8cm FlaK18 anti-aircraft guns set up in well emplaced positions in August 1944. As the front approached closer to Germany's borders, anti-aircraft units such as this were forced to evacuate these well prepared positions and become part of a mobile defense against both air and ground targets. These ones are painted dark sand and have white battery markings on the recuperator housing.

An 8.8cm FlaK 18 or 36 set up on a street in a Dutch city, September 1944. The camouflage and position of the gun suggest that they are prepared for a ground assault. The tall buildings would hinder its use in an anti-aircraft role.

A battery of 'Wespe' self-propelled guns mounting the 10.5cm IFH18M (M - mundungbremse - muzzle brake) howitzer, firing on enemy positions in southern Poland, early autumn 1944. Introduced in the spring of 1943, the 'Wespe' and 'Hummel' formed the backbone of the Panzer-Artillerie-Abteilungen. The photographer has caught them at the moment of firing - the three guns in the background are in full recoil.

Three Tiger I's from 1./s.Pz.Abt.506 travel down a muddy road in one of the towns in southern Poland in August 1944. They were resupplied with 45 new tanks in March and April 1944 in the Lemberg area. At this time, the battalion's tanks were marked with a large single or double digit tactical number on the forward side of the turret painted in white for 1.Kompanie and red and yellow for 2. and 3.Kompanie. The lead vehicle has the tactical number '6' and the third has the number '5' while the middle vehicle has no visible marking. The battalion lost all its tanks during the Soviet summer offensive against H.Gr.Mitte and was transferred to Germany for rest and refitting with the new Tiger II.

A Kfz.2 Schwimmwagen kicks up a cloud of dust as it races past an Sd.Kfz.251/1 Ausf.D north of Warsaw in September 1944. The half-track has a liberal covering of foliage draped on the front and sides for extra camouflage. Note that it is missing its MG shield.

Two Pz.Kpfw.IV Ausf.H or Ausf.J in a field near Warsaw in early September 1944. They may be from 19.Panzer-Division which, along with 3.Polizei-Panzer-Division and 5.SS-Panzer-Division 'Wiking', formed IV.SS-Panzer-Korps. This unit drove the Soviets from the city and back across the Vistula River, successfully holding back two Russian armies for almost two months.

A Tiger I sits broken down beside the road waiting for tow. Part of a small tactical number '2' is barely visible beside the open driver's hatch indicating it may be from s.Pz.Abt.502. The tank has been painted in a very distinctive camouflage pattern of green and brown over the dark sand base and appears to be a new vehicle.

A column from Panzer-Division 'Großdeutschland' marching through East Prussia, late September 1944. The leading vehicle is an Sd.Kfz.251/3 Ausf.D radio half-track with three antenna. They are for the FuG Spr f, FuG 5 and the star antenna for the FuG 8 radio sets. Following behind can be seen an NSU Kettenkraftrad, a pair of motorcycle combinations and a Schwimmwagen.

Since the middle of 1943, the Panzer-Divisions encountered an increasing amount of enemy air attacks as the Luftwaffe gradually lost control of the air. This in turn, created the need for more self-propelled anti-aircraft vehicles to protect the divisions. As the need grew desperate, many types of vehicles, along with specially developed Flakpanzers on obsolete tank chassis, were developed to carry the 2cm FlaK30 and FlaK38 anti-aircraft guns. Here we see a battery mounted on Opel Blitz 3-ton trucks, in September 1944, with quite elaborate two color camouflage schemes.

A late Tiger I fitted with steel wheels, ferrying troops of 21.Feld-Division (Luftwaffe) over the Venta River in Lithuania in late August 1944. The turret is turned to the rear revealing the tactical number '23?' painted in a location unique to vehicles of s.Pz.Abt.510. Another unique addition to note is the spare track link bar on the front of the hull with three segments. The battalion was formed in June 1944 and saw action mostly in the Baltic States and East Prussia.

Twenty-two new Pz.Kpfw.V Panther Ausf.G lined up in a field somewhere in Germany, early autumn 1944. These were probably among the last Panthers built with zimmerit coating which was ordered to be dropped on September 9, 1944. In the background can be seen several Sd.Kfz.251/9 Ausf.D half-tracks armed with the 7.5cm KwK37 L/24 gun.

A Pz.Kpfw.V Panther Ausf.G passes through the ruins of an East Prussian city in autumn 1944. There is no zimmerit on this vehicle indicating it was manufactured after the beginning of September 1944. It is also likely painted in red oxide primer with camouflage patches of green and dark sand that were now ordered to be applied at the assembly plants. The tactical number '322' is red with a white outline.

Two photographs of new late production Pz.Kpfw.IV Ausf.J from 5.Panzer-Division, involved in the battle for Goudap in October 1944. Two of the Pz.Kpfw.IV in the first photo, have the red devil's head emblem of Pz.Rgt.31 painted on a black rectangle on the front of the turret schürzen, while the tactical sign of the division, a yellow 'X' on a black square, can be seen painted on the rear of the turret schürzen in the other photo. The Balkenkreuz on it is also painted in an unusual manner with a white stencil outline around the black cross. The Balkenkreuz on the front of the turret schürzen visible in the first photo seems to be more of the conventional type and is followed by a large, white three digit tactical number which in this case, appears to be '733'. They are all painted in a classic ambush camouflage paint scheme.

Another Pz.Kpfw.V Panther Ausf.G makes its way through a heavily damaged city. The commander in his cupola and the loader, seen in the rear turret hatch, would not be so exposed if there was any danger from enemy snipers in the ruins and so the photo was probably taken during the retreat. Some of the missing side skirt armor can be seen stowed on the engine deck just in front of the exhaust pipes.

A late Pz.Kpfw.V Panther Ausf.G abandoned on a battlefield on the Eastern Front. The raised fan cover for the crew compartment heater, that was introduced in October 1944, can be seen on the engine deck although the vehicle is still fitted with the shielded exhaust pipes and not the 'flammvernichter' exhaust also introduced around the same time. The tactical number '239' is painted on the side of the turret in large red numbers with a white outline. Note the two penetrations in the 45mm thick rear plate of the turret.

German infantry, clad in winter camouflage uniforms, take up a position on a barren hill in southern Poland or Czechoslovakia in the late fall of 1944. They are supported by two old Russian T-26 tanks captured in 1941 and probably used for anti-partisan duty in the intervening years. The tanks have been repainted in dark sand paint and have large Balken crosses added to ensure they are not mistakenly identified by nervous German gunners. In the background, a pair of StuG.III Ausf.G assault guns can be seen on the road in the village.

After being almost totally destroyed in France during the summer of 1944, s.Pz.Abt.503 was re-equipped with 43 new Pz.Kpfw. Tiger Ausf.B at Paderborn in September 1944. The battalion was assembled for propaganda photographs before a few days of training and transportation to Hungary on October 12, 1944. Here the commander of 3.Kompanie in his Tiger with the tactical number '300' parades in front of the rest of the battalion lined up in review. His tank is painted in a classic three color camouflage scheme.

Most were painted in the standard three color camouflage scheme, but many were also painted in the new ambush scheme as well. At this time, only 3.Kompanie vehicles had received their three digit tactical numbers, painted in black with a white outline, but by the time the battalion reached Hungary, all of them had been marked.

The battalion moves out. Zimmerit was still applied in the factory until September 1944 and all their vehicles were covered with it. In readiness for transport by train, they have all been fitted with the narrow transport tracks. This must have been an awesome spectacle to see.

As the battalion leaves Paderborn, they pass a company of new Pz.Kpfw.V Panther Ausf.G which have not had zimmerit applied and have all been painted in the new ambush scheme.

Three Pz.Kpfw. Tiger Ausf.B from s.Pz.Abt.503 after their arrival in Hungary in October 1944. The one on the right is an older vehicle and does not have the spare track hangers on the turret introduced in June 1944. Part of the tactical number '2?0', painted in red with a white outline, can be seen under the pail hanging over the rear turret hatch.

Another Pz.Kpfw. Tiger Ausf.B of s.Pz.Abt.503 in Hungary, October 1944. Just to the left of the crewman leaning back against the turret, can be seen part of the first digit of the tactical number, a '3'. The vehicles would not remain in this pristine condition for long. After occupying the Citadel in Budapest, they were subordinated to 24.Panzer-Division and then 4.SS-Polizei-Panzer-Grenadier-Division for an attack on the Theiss River bridgehead.

StuG.III Ausf.G assault guns, Sd.Kfz.251/1 Ausf.D half-tracks and transport trucks from one of the SS-Panzer-Divisions, entrained for transportation to Hungary to take part in the Lake Balaton battles in February 1945. The StuG.III in the lower photo has concrete on the forward part of the roof of the fighting compartment for additional protection. A special mount has been attached to the MG shield for using the MG42 in an anti-aircraft role. It appears that the crew have painted eyes and eyebrows and possibly tusks on the topfblende mantlet which resembled a boars head.

A transport train loaded with vehicles of a Sturmgeschütz or Panzerjäger Battalion headed for the Eastern Front during the winter of 1944-45. A never ending stream of armored vehicles was sent to replace losses sustained in East Prussia, Silesia and Hungary in January 1945. In the foreground is an early Jagdpanzer IV Ausf.F armed with the 7.5cm PaK39 L/48 gun followed by a Jagdpanzer 38(t) Hetzer and several StuG.III Ausf.G.

Another Jagdpanzer IV Ausf.F on the Western Front in the winter of 1944-45. The German firm Vomag produced 769 of these vehicles from January to November 1944. In August 1944, they began installing the longer barreled gun, the 7.5cm PaK42 L/70, in some vehicles. The new version was designated Panzer IV/70(V) which had completely replaced the Jagdpanzer IV by December 1944. The schürzen have been modified slightly by the crew of this vehicle. It appears that the brackets have probably been damaged and removed, allowing the schürzen to be bolted directly to the bracket mounting lugs welded to the superstructure. The schürzen were then bent down at that point.

Two photographs showing the wreckage of two Luftwaffe 8.8cm FlaK18 anti-aircraft guns and one of their Sd.Kfz.7 half-track prime movers, demolished by the Soviet Air Force in February or March 1945 in the Graudenz area of East Prussia. Judging by the elevation on the guns and spent cartridges on the ground, they were able to put up some defensive fire before being destroyed. Both were painted in a camouflage pattern and had their position in the battery, 'A' and 'C', painted in white on the equilibrator housing in the standard fashion. Note the two different styles of gun shield. The half-track has the license number 'WL 477034'.

A destroyed Sd.Kfz.10 from the same Luftwaffe unit along with a wrecked motorcycle in the background. The body of one the unfortunate crew members can be seen laying in front of the half-track.

Three photographs of a column of soft-skin transport vehicles and a StuG.III Ausf.G destroyed in a Soviet bombing raid in the Torun area, early February 1945. The first photo is of an Opel Maultier that has been blown over onto its back, shedding its track and running gear in the violent explosion. In the second photo, the remains of an Opel Blitz can be identified while in the third photo, the StuG.III has been so completely destroyed as to be almost unrecognizable. Note the Russian soldier standing in the bomb crater next to the Opel Blitz.

A StuH 42 Ausf.G also destroyed in the same raid. This was a later model vehicle that was prepared for, but not fitted with, the remote control MG mount, but still fitted with side opening loader's hatches. These vehicles may be from a much photographed, but as yet unidentified, Sturmgeschütz-Abteilung that field modified the schürzen plates to hang from short pieces of pipe welded to angles attached to the mudguards. The modified brackets can be clearly seen. Note the 10.5cm casings littering the ground around the vehicle.

More demolished German soft-skin vehicles destroyed by the Soviet Air Force alongside the road near Torun. The Germans broke through the Soviet lines to escape encirclement and reached the banks of the Vistula River in February 1945, leaving much of their equipment behind. In the first photo, the Opel Blitz in the background had been painted in a winter camouflage scheme of thick, white lines over the old dark gray base. An illegible, shield shaped emblem has been painted on both doors. The closest vehicle has a Luftwaffe license plate number 'WL 111570'. The second photo is of a captured Soviet truck that has been incorporated in the Wehrmacht and has the license number 'WH-1094158'. Two bundles of fascines are still attached to the front bumper.

The wreckage of a Pz.Kpfw.IV Ausf.H in Kolberg in the spring of 1945. An internal explosion has blown off the transmission cover plate and driver's hatch and fire consumed the rubber from the roadwheels and return rollers. Note the unusual zimmerit pattern on the front plate of the superstructure.

Remains of German vehicles destroyed and abandoned in Gdynia or Sopot in the spring of 1945. On the right is an Sd.Kfz.7 half-track prime-mover with a very faintly legible 'WL' prefix on the license plate. Unfortunately, the unit emblems painted on the rear are not legible. This area of Poland became a graveyard to 4., 5., and 7.Panzer-Division, the latter of which was withdrawn to the west, surrendering to British forces at Schwerin in May 1945. 4. and 5.Panzer-Division continued to fight on, surrendering to the Soviets in April 1945.

A battery of 15cm Panzerwerfer 42 (Sd.Kfz.4/1) was abandoned on the Baltic coast near Gdynia in April 1945, after firing off all their ammunition. It appears to have been painted in a white winter camouflage which is badly deteriorating from high wave action from the Baltic Sea. A tactical number '3', probably painted in black, can be seen above the open middle bin door. Just over the driver's compartment, a 10.5cm lFH18(M) howitzer can be seen in the background.

Three photographs of abandoned German transport vehicles that were captured and put to use by the Polish Army during the final days of the war. The first one is a Ford V3000 3-ton truck which has seen long service in the Wehrmacht. It was painted in a dappled camouflage scheme on the wooden box only and appears to have been a civilian conscript as the former owners advertising still can be seen on the front of the canvas top. The next two show Sd.Kfz.7 half-track prime-movers that have been impressed into the Polish Army. Of special interest is the unusual fitting mounted to the back of one, the purpose of which is unknown.

A Soviet soldier poses on this nicely camouflaged Hanomag SS100N German Army tractor which has been abandoned on a flooded road near Berlin in May 1945. Besides the original camouflage, there are a number of markings painted on various parts of the vehicle. One, on the front mudguard, has been painted over and there is one, obscured behind the soldier's leg, painted on the door. A white circle with a number in it, is painted on the rear of the body, visible over the soldier's right shoulder and a white outline diamond with the letters 'An' is painted on the windscreen.

A battered Tiger I knocked out by the Russians near Berlin in April 1945, possibly from s.SS.Pz.Abt.503 which fought in that area. It has an interesting array of field modifications including a second, smaller stowage bin behind the standard bin, what appears to be motorcycle dispatch case fastened to the rear of the turret, a sheet metal rain guard over the mantlet and two jerrycan racks on the rear of the hull. The loader's periscope guard has been shot away and the zimmerit coating and lighter sheet metal parts have been peppered with shrapnel and small arms fire. In the background are two Tiger II that have also been knocked out. Just visible over the engine deck of the Tiger I is a large penetration in the nearest Tiger II's turret. Another photo of this vehicle appears on page 68 of 'Panzerwaffe at War (2) Moscow to Berlin'.

A late Pz.Kpfw.V Panther Ausf.G knocked out by the Polish Army in southern Germany during the last days of the war in May 1945. The anti-tank round penetrated the side of the hull just above the bottom of the sponson, blowing off the gun cleaning rod tube and part of the mudguard. Note that this Panther has foliage loops welded to the turret that were ordered to be installed starting in March 1945. Unusually, it still has the anti-aircraft MG rail welded to the cupola that was ordered dropped in January. The raised fan cover for the crew compartment heater can also be seen.

A totally destroyed Pz.Kpfw.V Panther Ausf.G, or possibly a Jagdpanther. The damage is too extensive to be sure. The early style of idler indicates that it was manufactured prior to October 1944, when the new, larger diameter self cleaning idler was introduced. It was destroyed by Polish forces in Germany in May 1945.

A StuG.III Ausf.G knocked out by the Polish Army near Dresden near the end of the war and pictured here during the summer of 1945. In one of the last battles of WWII, Field Marshall Ferdinand Schorner's Heeres-Gruppe Mitte, surrounded in Czechoslovakia, was ordered to break out and relieve Berlin. The attack was unsuccessful and resulted in the loss of many tanks and self-propelled guns on both sides. The crew of this StuG.III has attempted to improve the armor protection of their vehicle with additional armor plates and spare tracks on the side.

The order for the development of a vehicle mounting the 8.8cm PaK43 L/71 on the Panther chassis was issued on October 2, 1942. A year later, a wooden mock-up was shown to Hitler on December 16, 1943. Production of the Jagdpanther started in January 1944 and continued until March 1945. This late model Jagdpanther was captured by the Soviets and tested at their facility at Kubinka. It is painted in a late war camouflage scheme of brown and dark sand stripes over the dark green base that was authorized on December 20, 1944. The 'G' painted on the glacis may be a post-war Soviet marking.

A 38cm RW61 auf Sturmmörser Tiger, more commonly known as the Sturmtiger. There were 18 of these vehicles built from converted Tiger I hulls from August to December 1944. This vehicle was one of two used by the Germans during the Warsaw uprising and was captured by the Soviets afterwards. The bolted armor plate on the front of the hull and other details indicate that this was the prototype vehicle which was probably rushed to Warsaw for troop trials. It was evaluated by the Soviets after the war and is currently on display at the armor museum at Kubinka near Moscow.